# The Hermits of Dingle

*George Moore*

FUTURECYCLE PRESS

*www.futurecycle.org*

Published by FutureCycle Press
Hayesville, North Carolina, USA

ISBN 978-1-938853-21-0

# Contents

## 1. Wilderness

Learning to Swim................................................................9
The Cannibals..................................................................10
Teak............................................................................11
From a Short Distance....................................................... 12
Cúchulainn.................................................................... 14
Modern Articles of Faith....................................................15
The Greek Isle............................................................... 16
Ice Hut....................................................................... 20
River Ice..................................................................... 21
The Hermits of Dingle....................................................... 22
The Monk's Body...............................................................23
Hagiography...................................................................24
Hands on the Wall............................................................ 25
A Geography of Heights....................................................... 26
Death Valley................................................................. 27
Trails.......................................................................28
The Most Remote Prison in the World......................................... 30
The First Music.............................................................. 31
Ride......................................................................... 32
The Real Thing............................................................... 33
Survivor Suite...............................................................34
The Far Side of Heaven....................................................... 36
The Old Man of Hoy........................................................... 37
Off the Coast of County Kerry................................................ 38
The Language School.......................................................... 39
The Poet's Hand.............................................................. 40
The Poem Talks Back.......................................................... 41

## 2. The Cities

The Sacred City.............................................................. 45
A Night in the Life.......................................................... 46
In Another Country........................................................... 47
Kathmandu....................................................................48
The Dali Café................................................................ 49
Subways in Europe............................................................ 50
Capela dos Ossos.............................................................51

The Poet's Place................................................................52
The Monkey Temple...........................................................53
The Dogs of Calcutta.......................................................... 54
On the Death of Other People............................................55
Junk..................................................................................... 56
Finishing Work................................................................... 57
Respect for the Dead...........................................................58
Inside Wat Pho....................................................................59
Desert Fathers..................................................................... 60
Reburial............................................................................... 61
The Irony Miner.................................................................. 62
The Colossus of Rhodes....................................................... 63
Running............................................................................... 64
Behind the Houses Under Construction............................. 66
Gallarus Oratory, Dingle..................................................... 67
The Call............................................................................... 68
The Other Side.................................................................... 70
Last Chance Café................................................................. 71
The Butterfly Effect............................................................. 72
Mystic Renovations............................................................. 73
Diorama............................................................................... 74
Watching the Trains............................................................ 75
Landscapes........................................................................... 76
Last Gas for A Thousand Miles...........................................77
Returning............................................................................. 78

Acknowledgments............................................................... 81

"In the life of each of us, I said to myself,
there is a place remote and islanded, and given to
endless regret or secret happiness; we are each the
uncompanioned hermit and recluse of an hour or a day;
we understand our fellows of the cell to whatever age
of history they may belong."

—Sarah Orne Jewett, *The Country of the Pointed Firs*

# 1. Wilderness

*But I'll tell you what hermits realize. If you go off into a far, far forest and get very quiet, you'll come to understand that you're connected with everything.*

*—Alan Watts*

## Learning to Swim

We spent time underwater like falling,
the sandy shore of the local pool
baked us clean, dark, invisible but
so terribly visible, the body never ascending
or descending, nothing but the sun stalled
for what seemed the eternity of an instant.

You dove in to save me. I spurted up chlorine
and blue, that icy blue of swimming pools,
of false bottoms, of the first taste of fear.

We spent time together floating on the surface
of things, once in awhile talking about God
or the inevitability of death,
pockets left in the water where you dropped a stone,
but only words in the end, sand and words.

I was dark as a coffee bean
and yet could not get the summer into me,
it would not feed me what I needed desperately,
salty water, and the way things evaporate.

Now the spaces are singular, warped
like that stone resting on the fabric of space,
drawing me back into an invisible hole
where time spent was and is still there,
your turquoise suit, my black hair
shining through the momentary waves of heat.

# The Cannibals

*—for MS, at Fossil Butte*

A fish in a fish's mouth is rare,
but one caught in another's jaws
between the limestone plates
of this ancient lake,
now turned to stone,
is a miracle,
and not one dependent on time
hammered out with the wisdom of a god,
but on the moment as moments will
come and go for their own eternity,
and however long it lasts for these
hungry creatures alone,
for us it is the blink of the eye.

The fish that the fish ate
was a meal in the link of a hungry chain,
locked into its circling existence,
and the fish that ate, itself was eaten
in another time and another place,
and in another stone
perhaps preserved,
its life captured in an image of vitality
with someone else standing,
contemplating the limits of a universe
that serves itself up as a meal
like a slice of meat between two stones
which sandwich all eternities.

# Teak

The wide, long table, cut from a single tree,
the monks say was worth more than they eat
in five years, more rice and fruit and fungus,
a delicacy, more than any would ever need.

The tree was split down the middle,
forty feet long, polished by the monks who
know the meaning of movements, of hard work,
of the process of rendering a tree humanly useful.

We did not pray for the food but for ourselves,
that we should be rescued from a life of greed,
desire, for three hundred thousand dollar trees, stolen
by Thai soldiers from Burmese borderlands.

The temple was silent at the edge of the caves,
almost like a ship on the sea in calm weather,
but the ships whose decks stripped these forests clean
were never really transported anywhere

beyond their moment, which I think of now
in terms of trees, of the life cycles of the jungles,
of travel, of how we are here, and of the one-way
voyage of this ancient teak.

# From a Short Distance

*—for John Eisele, in memoriam*

At the start of the year, no one could say
what would be found in that stretch
through spring, the tearing away of time,

as loss does not segment itself like a worm
to grow back into wholeness somewhere
in another life. No one chooses the image

that remains, the year a heap of seconds,
or which day will crystallize into all days,
the crucible for an alchemy of brothers.

I heard you were back in, on my way north,
the bike running through open desert like
a knife, my life built on that kind of thing.

But I turned south, shifted down to meet
the coastal rains, ran for two days, and
was carried only into the next moment.

What was left to do was nothing really,
the deck of the boat needed oiling, the
ducks out back feeding, your sons

needed another year or two. But you and I
were more often at the head of the storm,
your father's second wife, my mother's

second husband, two teenage sons
similarly different, light-years apart but
through a space that was curved the same.

What we want and what we find are two
different worlds, and you lived well in both.
The sea was on hold, sliding along beside

the crash of things, that noise seemed so
unnatural then, a sound like total destruction.
The needle read out at eighty and I moved

across a membrane of time that separates
the living and the dying, that last-minute
consciousness of having been, and the one

that still pretends the world will wait forever.
It didn't, and yet our thread was already spliced
in a way that separate seconds did not matter.

# Cúchulainn

*The Hound of Ulster*
                    —*Táin Bó Cúailnge*

I name the dog
after a Celtic hero,
in a reversal of sympathies.
Here the dog becomes the man
who was the Hound of Ulster,
the quickest and most powerful
chieftain of his times.

Reversed, the myth makes him
equal to ten men, makes him kill
the beast before the door of the great hall,
when he himself was only ten.

But my dog obeys no commands,
does what animals do when they are
fearless, half wild, he runs away
to have his own adventures.

The cattle run through the neighbor's pasture,
the deer stir by the creek bed and flee,
other dogs call out in their mournful
brotherhood.

But it is really I who have changed,
reversed the myth of the society of dogs,
dug up old tales and rumors
of Cúchulainn's famous cattle raid in the north,
of the great brown bull he stole,
he who is my Celtic echo,
thief, night hunter, myth reversed
in the dawn when I walk my dog.

## Modern Articles of Faith

Inside cragged walls of a ruined church, boys are
kicking a ball where a king once crowned his son,
telling him, *showing mercy will not save you.* By our time,

only the yard around the cathedral walls remains,
and we hump history through the broken arms of doors,
to stone breastplates of sarcophagi worn nameless,

though a pamphlet says another king was born, died, before
the church followed. Spaces now open to the sky.
The ball rolls to a stop before our feet and dies,

as shouts go up through the hobbled choir, half-fallen
archways once hung with heavy tapestries,
and now the sounds of boys screaming decrees.

With evening, the ghosts arrive. The son beheaded
by his father, the king, when there was talk
of treason. I snap a shot of the ruptured cupola

as night creeps in. It's too cool for this season,
but the grass has come to life, as ramparts fall to darkness,
and the boys pick up their ball and head for home.

## The Greek Isle

It was not memory,
at the time, but love
of the absent,

water's way, an ocean
keeping up the pace
unfashioned in its

contingencies, those
life conditions, suspended
before responsibilities.

Cavafy's youthful
complications, the same
figure leaving a line

in the sand, reaching
into a common ocean,
where love displaces

the future needs
so completely, as if
this *this* was all.

Now I must remember,
as it is not today, forced
back into some pattern

that was not there,
the beaches so
empty, whitewashed

houses few, in-between
cafés with rickety
tables. What I said

was not meant
to be remembered,
or gathered later as

summary, sensibility,
anymore than written,
signed. How easy

it is to fashion the past,
play new stones
off its still surfaces,

as he did, making
his loves untouchable
histories.

We forget to find
memories again,
lend them substance

in word or phrase,
material signs, signing
what the universe

has carried off,
discarded, pure
energy, dispersed as

atoms shed electrons,
then discover virtual
otherness, hiding, throw

it off so that it creates
out of itself another self,
another moment.

The writer knew this
transfiguration, mulled
into a pure absence.

But not that one,
never that one there,
as you see it, that shade

touching half a table,
so hot you grew visible
in the sun, an older woman

in black, pulling back
the body skin
of a butchered rabbit.

What do we learn
from ourselves?
Circles we enter

and leave, sights
on horizons, sound
emporiums, for me,

the unfiltered Crete
sifted down through
three dozen years?

Little perhaps
that we do not create,
out of the variable need

to fulfill the silent
craving of here,
these people

we have become.
Not at the end
of lines but as lines

woven into ropes
that might hold ships,
or carry cargo aloft,

swinging the past
before our eyes,
marked fragile

in our own red print.
Looking north
out of Alexandria,

he would see this
space that is other
and self, unmarked,

displaced for a time,
or a lifetime, curled
back into love

that is fragile
and permanent
as pillar stone.

## Ice Hut

Ice hut on the white,
fire in a can
at the feet of a freezing
netherworld, the fish
like ghost streams,
streamers of ghosts,
voices in the frozen dawn,
the voiceless coming up
out of the thick skein,
rivulets locked in this
other time,
the can settling into
its own impression,
hand on the line,
out historied,
unhistoried, no time
past or present
but this simple sacrifice,
limbs as aware as eyes,
body double,
doubts drowned in
solid, turbid air,
fish first, and then hand,
molecules of the moment,
out of still-life, evolution.

# River Ice

The river cracks
in syllables, impossible
to say that here we step
but once, for with ice
the river sways,
buckles back upon itself,
and bleeds its own
universe of words. Across
the icy way from where
Niagara Park ends,
other children are
staring into our void.
They challenge us,
each other, testing fear
for its power of renewal.
A half-mile perhaps,
this white street of glass,
a field that suddenly
contracts. You hear it
give up winter ghosts;
beneath it our worlds
do not exist, the cold
too cold to imagine.
For us, the Arctic begins
right here, the next
Ice Age. Out past where
our mothers will say
was good sense, we
chance our way.
These words themselves
might shift, weather
already warming,
and with our retreat
only the water beneath
is moved to wave.

## The Hermits of Dingle

Nothing but rock and gannet guano,
and the sparse kinds of grasses that cling

to the inevitable, and cliff edges gouged
by bluster and cold Irish sea, and this

beauty, stark as a shelled moon. The *clocháns*,
beehive huts, coned in dry stone masonry,

no *cill* to hide in from the *gaoth* blown up
from the fuming coves, and here

to contemplate the will of God,
and one's own will's failure, comprehend

how the taste of nothing can sate
a restive anima that has fed on worlds

and gained no weight, light as a shearwater
or kittiwake, fix-winged, afloat on lifts

of anonymous air. And how in time
the eye-length of the world runs a course

from Skellig rooks to shore, and back,
interminably, and white-capped rocks

at lantern's edge bead to a focal point
and score the night as on a living stone.

# The Monk's Body

was taken from his cell,
where he lay down to rest
during the thin hours of his last night,
and dismembered by the best of his friends,
the righteous ones,
who had come into his life at first as farmers,
working for years in the hardened fields
before entering the monastery above the town
and giving their lives over to the incredible,
as if they were pollen carried in a stream.

Then the parts of his body
are carried higher up the plateau,
and there the animals and birds devour him,
as if he were a sacred meal prepared by the monks,
the righteous ones,
for their other selves,
the ones they will come someday to be,
or the ones they were before.

And when there are only bones,
the bones are ground to a fine meal
and baked with flour and yeast,
and made into bread,
and the loaves are broken and scattered
across the plateau for the birds
who return to finish off the monk,
who enters their small stomachs
like pieces of a dream.

And his friends,
the righteous ones,
hear the songs of the birds
and hear the sounds of the night around them,
and wait in the darkness of their cells
for the final passage toward their own migrations,
knowing they will be blood and gristle,
and transformed too, if they are lucky,
into the energy of wings.

# Hagiography

*—after Cavafy*

The poet turns obscure
through a haze of hagiographers
because of the worship of idols
other than men. That a poetry is grand,
eloquent and ironic, means nothing
to the strict reader of words. Ideas are
only a disguise for homoerotic flourishes,
stealthfully uncovered. History
does better to forget
than let its insects feed on pages
where life is indistinguishable
from regret. Hard lies
are better than a soft truth, however
soft the seasons in ancient Alexandria.
The truth is, love transcends the senses,
engenders its own distinction, rises above
the taste for animal flesh, or the traffic
in black extremes of European cities.
These things are real as words,
hard little signs that refuse to see
or forget another's heaven.

# Hands on the Wall

*El Morro National Monument, New Mexico*

These are children's markings
perhaps, or shaman's, who can say?

The white outlines of human
extremities, made plain by contrast.

The mark of the man, a woman,
a child who was one or both at times,

growing into the place where
parents had cut the trail.

We see the cross, the wavy line
of a river, and feet walking a path,

and know someone came before,
and came through a different time,

marking the measure of themselves,
and their way into the future.

Our way into their past is here,
in our hands on their hands

on the reddish rock, we feel this
something in ourselves, this

sudden human need to sign
and set the future trail.

# A Geography of Heights

Escaping America, I go west
into Tibet, up Everest as far as lungs can carry me,
looking for that back door to heaven.

It is strange, the way we praise high peaks,
the Buddhists leave prayer flags on each natural rise,
as if the gods stepped lightly from mount to mount

and never touched the valleys. And I climb,
sometimes for the simple pleasure of saying
*I have climbed,* or for the airy borderland,

the stratosphere as much of mind as matter,
even as the Sherpas shuffle up and down
without a thought. The Chinese stop three of us

before Camp #1; for a fee we might climb on.
But then how would it sound? From Base Camp
we went on, further into the unknown,

but not far enough to look back down,
only to where we felt the movement of the glaciers.
That's the reality of earth time, a sheet of ice

saying something we do not want to believe,
that everything moves, and to reach a summit
is to be just beyond yourself, a step further

than yesterday, out on a plain, or in the city,
on a less urgent day, when you hear the roar
of surf, and stretch out on the sand.

## Death Valley

Words grow thick
with storms of dust here,
a history imagined where
worse lies ahead, when,
cast into hell,
there is a crossing,
blind, as bats in the sun.
Homesteaders wishing
to be out of the devil's
heartland. The senses
may say otherwise,
play the mind with smells,
distances that cannot be
remembered quite,
or forgotten, mixed in
with flashy spring. Light blue
miniatures of desert buds.
Beavertail cacti
bleed scarlet along a rutted
chunk of pavement, no word
could ink a stain that way,
the heat rising. Death
is a word that refuses ends,
spurs the mind on to spring,
cannot be contained.
Then Desert Lupine
or Royal Robed Chias
bring it home again.
The name clings
to a man's brain,
and yet cannot flower
like the valley, breaks
open, rather, in its frying pan.
Dazzling colors of the dead,
and the highway finally
loops back upon itself
like infinity.

## Trails

Once there were few trails.
Nothing led anywhere. People
wandered aimlessly into places
they had never seen. Soon,
however, the idea of traversing
the curved surface of this rock
turned into a perpetual fever,
and the same people began
to wander toward something
they could not understand.
They made trails to cover
their tracks, made trails to be
sure they were going somewhere,
made trails to show others
they knew exactly what
they were doing, and then
justified each of their efforts
by maps. They made trails
like deer make trails, a hundred
spidery webs crisscrossing
a hillside, out of laziness,
out of indecision. They made
trails into the deepest heart
of darkness, into the world's
recesses, into others' territory.
The trails were proud things,
built by newly graduated
engineers. They drained and
sloped, and climbed and traversed
perfectly. They were the work
of industrious men, wanting
to leave their mark. Their mark
was the trail, the secret scar
on the open space, its strategic
division of land into quadrants,
of wilderness into klicks.
Of course, the trail ended
in the heart, it was a spear

thrown by the industrious
at the open and unmarked.
It was an arrow shot without
thinking at the insomniac's foot.
The weapon of the suburbs.
The false dream of those
who have lost direction,
and seek its remnants in trails
that will take them anywhere
away from where they are.

## The Most Remote Prison in the World

The young guide says he's slipped out a few times,
he's maybe twenty-two or -three, made his way
across the high routes the Dalai Lama himself once took
into northern India, through the impassable Himalayas,
"the top of the world," out of Chinese hands.
But he has nowhere to go, he says; he's trapped
in a neighboring country just as much as at home.
His vision of the modern world is Srinagar, and once, Delhi.
He smiles and says he would like to see it all, the world,
would learn to speak in many languages. He is hungry
for my English, does not want me to practice my Chinese,
does not want even his own Tibetan, has come to see
his homeland as a prison. I think of Buddhist travelers
to Tibet, the tourists who come to find some spiritual truth,
who buy and trade and learn to speak Chinese,
and perhaps forget the pilgrimage Buddhism itself made,
up from the Ganges River valley over the high plateaus,
into the minds of this country of lamas. It's often forgotten
that Tibet once ruled China, on and off for centuries.
But some also forget that we live in a shrinking world
where to stay ignorant on command means a prison,
sure as the ones of thick mud walls and iron bars:
my guide's sense of the world from deep within it.

# The First Music

The first music was an accident, the clanging of a stone
against the resonance of solid tree, the slipping of rocks downstream
in high season, some impossible whining of old-growth limbs
pushed up against their leaning neighbors.

The ear picked it up almost coincidentally, at first, a haunting,
something the brain said but did not say. A pattern was born
out of a longing to mimic an appearance of the wind
at the back of the mind.

So was the first moment of music a moment of human anticipation,
of humanity, a sudden rush of synchronicity, the sleeping
senses electric with a newborn synesthesia,
circling the heart within the animal skin.

Words would follow, but not for ages. At first, it was just the noise
of living, a river speaking in tongues, stones mumbling their way
down long glacial corridors; it was cave echoes, wordless shouts
from god-high cliffs; it was the mimic of birds trading names, wolves

lamenting the disappearance of night, long-silent elk in throaty rut.
The words at first did not matter because it was the body
performing its rites, coaxing light from darkness, tending fires
to keep the heavens alive.

Music was grieving, as voiceless as the disappearances among us.
Without leaving tree or stream, it entered the living
and the dead, those who come back as if they were the very singing,
and the cave dwellers, aware the earth itself was their mouth.

## Ride

I ride across the open grasslands
east, up from Greeley to the frontier,
headed back. I pass through towns
that are no longer more than boarded

farm houses, shuttered-up single stores,
the empty silo of a grain elevator.
The Pawnee might have made this into
something more, these tough grass hills.

I ride through the open window
of a world where time moves back
and forth.  It's strange to be astride
the bike at 70 mph and smelling sweat

off the roped mane of a horse. But
there are ghosts, and then there are ghosts.
The air thins into poorer shields
against an immutable universe.

I ride before the evening rhumb
is complete—a few flatbeds rolling east,
empty, as wheat fields return to prairie—
and see the quiet explode, replete

with the highway's crumpled forte lace,
before the purer forms of growth
renegade again, grasses sweeping clear
to the border, into re-opened range.

## The Real Thing

No matter how old you get
the real thing waits.

It might be a matter of days
or years. It might be the next

century. The real thing
inhabits the spaces you create

with your eyes closed,
with your insides out.

And for that reason
it remains invisible to you,

beyond the reach of eyes
and ears, beyond the mind's

greediness for inclusion, eluding
the fullness of absolute being.

The real thing does not confuse
so much as it shapeshifts

when confusion intrudes.
You have it but you have it not.

It escapes you but it is you.
The years roll by unnoticed

until one day, suddenly, coming
upon yourself, unafraid, you find

you've been waiting all along
in the middle of the real thing.

## Survivor Suite

Phoenix hotel zone density
thins to the razorwire playgrounds

Aztec Bride
My Tuxedo
a motel for the first night
next to Faith North School

Running easy, Hohokam
canals running beneath
these desert-clean streets

Garfield historic district
gravel yards

artificial turf
chain-linked corner lots

a man squatting
no, a sago palm

crossing the sunken freeways
invisible to the empty streets

the bungalows on half-acre lots
broad boulevards for avenues

sunshine strips the wide arteries
of fear, the quiet morning light
penetrates time, that

disabler
wakes a line of identical
doors slowly

a man cleans out his car
soft Mexican crooner sings
from his half-dozen bassy speakers

four men shift feet in a yard
around a grill, Hatch chilies roast

in Saturday morning stillness

aged hippies laugh out loud
from a bench, one
gray black beard
glistens in last night's dew

as trees, the Bradford pear
mock snow in white bud glean
in the desert heat of streetlights

the city still slow to wake
slow all day in the heat

echoes a primal urge to be nowhere
dissolving amid long grids of even streets

seeing the old golden waters
Yavapai to Camelback
and White Tank mountains

a landscape of railroads and mines

John Birch mumbling
in his drink, to waken
evangelicals

turning right and right again
territorial capital, awkward lean towers

Chase Westward Ho Sheraton skyline
high-rise fountain in an arid land

surviving the extremes
of planted oasis
crime kings and beasts of burden

and out on a Saturday morning
the pre-heat sympathies
of an old woman led by a dog

and children playing in a jet stream
from a cracked yard hose.

# The Far Side of Heaven

*Nós ossos que aqui estamos pelos vossos esperamos*

From somewhere out there, the bones ring like wind-chimes against
the prevailing storm. Looking out into the darkness, the eyes are the
problem, unequipped for the absolute, ready to read any sparkle of
iridescent light. Without seeing what the dead see, looking backward
into us, we go on hoping for the worst. But we have mistaken the dead;
they have no desires. They care less about what is left behind than we
do, who have not left anything behind. Less than the loose hinge of
a screen door, or the wind in the grass over the prairie. If the dead
believe in anything, they believe in death as the in-between. We of the
here and now are not part of this. The others are coming behind, they
say, no matter, coming but always suspended, like virtual particles
hanging on the edge of a black hole. The bones of the living are like
the bones of the dead, only less brittle, more imaginary. On the High
Alentejo in Portugal, there is a chapel abandoned to the sheep and cattle.
The sanctuary is filled with the droppings of beasts, and the windows
are broken out, as if the last were searching for perpetual daylight.
And on the chapel's side, above a small forgotten yard of headstones,
a tile in the style of the last great religious age, reads, *Our bones lie here,
waiting for yours.* Some say, in the end, there are no echoes, only the
breath that you cannot exhale.

# The Old Man of Hoy

The sea stack
off Orkney Island,
bent like an old man,
plume-haired in surf
to skirt his knees,
is earth old, and
failing. Now base-
jumped and iron-
mongered. The ferry
tilts in acquiescence
to the slant of galaxy,
autos slide side to side
and into your gut,
in the great belly
of the beast, metal
beneath slamdancing.
On the third deck,
the gunnels rise
and fall though
three stories up,
meet grey matter
of a watery world
like a wall of stone.
Sea and sky fuse
to gunmetal, and this
surface, a double-edged
Gaelic claymore
held above our heads,
is the Old Man's
crumbling cliff blade.
And as my breath
is crushed to pulp
and stomach churns,
the earth echoes back
the voyage of our
brief achievements.

## Off the Coast of County Kerry

Skellig Michael rests a good distance
off the Iveragh shore, a sheer stone isle

tangled in gannet guano, threading hairs
of mist from seas that do not settle down

but whip the world into a foam, a
God anger. Now humans crawl its sides,

steep slate steps, cut by monks, inviting death,
as when the monks lived there in *clocháns*

a thousand years. But today the dead
are remembered in suits, safety first,

history obscured. The oratory terrace,
a far reach into the clouds, where heaven

waits for the unprepared, unexpected
dangers of a mortal world, ringing meditative

beehive cells, the burial *leacht*,
like a noisy circle of birds.

# The Language School

In a basement,
of what was the chapel
in an old cloister, before
God reorganized the nuns
into city dwellers, I found
a manuscript of impossible
visions, recorded by an angel,
or child, in what looked
like blood, but perhaps
was the ink thickening
in my own arteries.

The language
was one of sighs. I held
the book out and listened
to the distillation of traffic
outside, the background
voices of energy hitting
pistons, turning wheels
in thin songs.

On a chalkboard,
in one of the many rooms above
without windows, I mapped out
the nouns and verbs
of the interaction of angels
with humans, and found
no sign sufficient for
the past exchange.

But the place was empty
and I was alone.
What was spoken there,
on the many floors of
the old monastery, was
a language I didn't know
which had fastened itself
to the darkness and silence,
waiting to break open
on the altar stone.

## The Poet's Hand

is old and cramped;
he finds it easier to use his teeth
to hold the pen, his head moves

to make amends. It sways
with the breeze more easily today
than in the past. His strokes seem

to last a bit longer. Like Zen,
the brush or pen does not so much
matter as the mark left by the trail

of its own design, both ignited
and then extinguished by degrees.
He sees the poem better

this close to the page. If his teeth
will last, perhaps he'll be able to kiss,
or even eat, the things he sees.

That's always been the point—
the poem a sort of map, his moves
always a preparation for the feast.

## The Poem Talks Back

The Other always stays away
on Mondays. The child listening to a voice
through a tin can on a long string,
warping time from other planets in other galaxies.

The poem whistles rudely, coughs,
says there must be an end to this
fumbling about in our sleep, searching for
a child who has died but has not ceased to be.

The poem's blind. But that's the point, after all,
of language. It rides down the middle ground,
ignoring traffic, screaming from the windows,
something about its efforts at survival.

Can you make out what it says? It accuses
all of us, wanting to scale things down
to the possible, to find a hiding place
where the child remembers what was in his head.

But not how the day began or ended.
Things always emerge as rough adults, with eyes
blank and milky. Enough to be awakened by
this face, pulled on like a well-worn cap.

# 2. The Cities

*New York has more hermits than will be found in all the forests, mountains and deserts of the United States*

*—Simeon Strunsky*

## The Sacred City

Beneath the dome of the great believers, people wander night and day.
Full of the dead, the spirits cannot escape. Who'd go back if they
thought desire would live in another place than among the lingering?
The first impression, not of blue, but of tiny signatures of tiles in the
wheel of the dome. In a symmetry, mosaic and unprofaned, the center
of the sacred city. Beggars on wheels-and-boards with padded palms,
in a hierarchy of human decay. A legless fellow smiles from his
command post at the head of a line at the main gate. Couples with
cameras talk of hopeless degradation, and designs constantly swimming.
How brittle is the difference we call everyday. Blood reds and blues in
intricate mosaics, are they a thousand eyeless reaches of the spirit?
A man takes up his cup, rolls off toward his veiled home, a crack in the
universe. Does he feed a wife, a child, wait for the blessed subterranean
heaven of sleep? Is he more than a survivor, among survivors, in the
sacred city?

## A Night in the Life...

*Dublin billboard, Summer 2005*

There's a car burning
without reason. No war
now, no riots, but the riot
of the heart. The colonizers
inhabit, cohabit. But it's
not a momentary thing
that sets a car afire.
No, the car burns in
a brilliant aftermath of love
for nothing, in the trap
of the moment, created
in the vacuum of a generation
forgetting. What was lost
on a Dublin street that summer
was the point, the next step,
the meeting in some kind
of heaven, here, where
the land is still an ardent green.
The billboard blames
adolescent chaos.
The drunken soldiery abed,
the kids throw bottles
at the stars, and kill
a pedestrian gentleman
of some night-shade color.
They call it a night on the town.
Old timers say it's youth
in need of some release.
But history simmers
like a drop of blood
in a holy font.

## In Another Country

the brother's life is nowhere as ridiculous
as his death, autopsied by mistake, a coroner

himself. The postmodern age. Riding down
from Oregon along the coast in torrential rain,

the motorcycle struggles to deliver me whole
before his end, but he is faster than I am,

wasting away. There are many things
in the world that are unfair, and death is only

a shadow of them all. We hiked to Ouzel Lake
and laughed at how much our feet hurt,

blistered through years, separated, singled out
each for his own trail. The wife who died

of arthritis, the St. Helen's dead, the cult suicides
of Heaven's Gate. His worlds were split in two

and I inhabited the better one. And now I'm
left in this other country, coming down a coast

again, where to one side of me is all the flux
of life, and on the other, a foreign country.

## Kathmandu

Back before the neon city,
when cars blew by you in a fit of dust,
when trees were thin as pencil lead
(but there were trees), and stupas warped
for centuries in monsoon swelling heat,
still held together with hand-forged nails,
there was a hostel off Pie Street,
where foreigners always moved through
various states of meditation, transmigration,
bubbles of consciousness, around
the winter solstice and Christmas that year.
At the U.S. Embassy, they served us scotch
with ice, the taste forgotten for a year,
served up for transient trippers
like children at a poor man's knees,
and said this was the American thing to do,
to bless those who the rest of the world left
forgotten in infected, Indian prisons,
or trapped at borders whenever the war
with Pakistan renewed. Seasonal greetings.
But it was something anyway.
And more than the cold room,
washing my hair in an icy tap,
and curling tight in a thin bag
to sleep out December's failing light.
The scotch warmed, silk
soaked in the smoke of a wood fire,
an old scarf around my inner core.
And the sleeper awoke, the season revealed,
all in the smile of a Buddhist hearing
an Embassy staffer's joke. That was
the first Christmas away. Now,
every one not home returns me to the East,
to the cold that was a cure for the season's
isolation. To that brief contact with others.
As clear a moment in my mind
as the single candle heating the hostel room.

## The Dali Café

The crowds are not rushing the gates
of the golden temple, nor are the eggs
in danger of falling off the battlements.
*But you can't get a decent cup of coffee here,*
I hear from someone in a flowered shirt
(one the Maestro himself would abhor),
blossoming from a tiny aluminum patio chair.
Women in black wear startling jewelry
yet smaller than the best kept masterpieces
of the museum's auxiliary store. An old car
propped up in the nuns' courtyard,
a museum now with glassed-in out-of-doors,
was never so old before. Each second
of art melts again, each hand of the clock
seems distorted anew. We have traveled
the rich landscape of Spain, Franco's fascists
all gone into hiding, with the artist
now dappled a duller gray, to arrive
at the gates of the fabulously mendacious,
whose crimes will go unnamed.

## Subways in Europe

I ride out into nowhere, just to ride
the Paris Red Line. Because...
it's Paris, after all. And riding is being
anywhere but home, on a bus, riding west.
There are those who think riding the subways
of Europe only a way to get around,
to work or the theater, to a bookstore
or any destination, with a purpose,
a goal. But I ride for the pleasure
of the displacement. Distance grows in me
like a nervous worm. No one rides
the subways here just to ride.
They believe in destiny.

I ride through factory towns
on the outskirts of industrial cities,
through neighborhoods where I find
incomprehensible graffiti, screaming words
whipped up out of a maelstrom of urban
malaise, languages of the super-real,
the non-subtle, the terminally left behind.

I ride through tracks of subsistence gardens
built on the edges of railway lines,
plots that feed those who cannot ride the subways
for pleasure. It is a time machine, this urban train,
journeying back into the world's finest,
forgotten ancestries. It is the web of a spider
that feeds on my desire for the
oldest forms of communication.

## Capela dos Ossos

A space full of bones, the monks' map
of the next world, or the world as they see it, here,
among the ephemeral, the fragile, the mothers

whose children have disappeared. *No children's bones
were used in the construction of this chapel*
the sign reads. We believe in an even chance.

Light low as the meditative atmosphere of a tomb,
but with a thousand femurs, a thousand more elbows,
a hundred ripened skulls. The walls draped out

in death, old death, ancient sensibilities, finding
our way along a broken world, grave by grave. Then
suddenly, in the street again, the unmapped day

infused with sunlight. This hidden nave, Évora,
Portugal, farms sprouting new wheat, olive orchards,
sunflower and oilseed. The lane leads slowly back to life.

## The Poet's Place

Some say the poet's place is in the city,
washing himself in the human lees,
the dirt men make that does not blow away.

Some say the poet's place is in the snowy fields,
watching as the blackbirds cross a winter day,
making out that this is their eternity.

Some say the poet's place is on a mountaintop,
like the sage, living alone out in some cave,
and knowing God as a lover.

I say the poet's place is here under a stone
on the first page, a salamander sleeping in the mud
that daylight startles and night rescues.

Others will say the poet's place is at the head
of the class, an actor on a stage, rehearsing
the beauty he might have seen.

But the poet's real place is here in the language,
sleeping under the flat, round word, turning
in the curve of another's ear.

## The Monkey Temple

Drawn to that other image of Creation,
marauder monkeys beneath Swayambhu's sleepy eyes
attack a dog and leave it with its face swollen,
soon to die. It stumbles

toward a dumb eternity. With head distended,
a hollow stone, blood ballooning, it wobbles
through a favorite temple like a drunken god,
blind with a kind of ravaged wisdom.

At times, the monkeys attack a child
on the great ascent, snatch it from its mother's arms,
to leave it infected with a seer's madness
at the gates of animal heaven.

No one notices when the dog curls up
and no longer whines. But in the wind, a child
dances, rattling chain-link curtains on desecrated shrines
to discover the Buddha, sweeping with bundled straw.

## The Dogs of Calcutta

do not live long, no longer than the children
or men in their thirties who lie down in frozen sleep,
no longer than the women who give birth to a world
only to leave it with a breath like the flower of a blessing,
no longer than rats, or cats, as they are all of one population,
but do they live as long as a young man traveling
across air-conditioned deserts, through cresting waves
on even keels, through the air in the silent, turbo darkness?
For no good reason on earth is his life longer than theirs.

## On the Death of Other People

They are always going,
coming and going, into and out of,
always there in the rearview mirror
or in a passing flash of recognition
along the side of a road.
They treat you like you were special,
awkwardly so, and like your heart
was just another organ, a plump
little cherry in the middle
of their solar system.
The effect is always as
after a storm, the wheat fields
flattened, the fences torn up,
and the windows echoing
in an ancient rattle.
They take a piece of fleshy something
with them, some living that leaves
its hole, a space you are left
to inhabit, in the air above
their quiet ground.
But worst of all, they die before you,
sucking out the world into a point,
a singularity, a questionable quantum
interface, drinking your blood
to keep their memory alive.

## Junk

In Tihar prison, outside Delhi, the white boys passed the needle around.
We all have hepatitis, a voice said, so it doesn't matter. They drank the
open channel water, might as well, another said, a blithe neglect on the
avenue to self-destruction. The guards were always ready too, who could
pass up such beauty? The longhairs needed only the spoon for meals,
and for dancing. It was better here, one said, than out there in monsoon
country. No one spoke the language. But in there, the language was
universal. I brought something to smoke, but they told me a needle was
worth a thousand goddamn *bidis*. When not up, they were edged like
rough glass. When I get out I'll head up north to see the Dalai Lama.
My mother's wondering where the hell I've got to out of London.
I wrote six months ago but they'll never get it. I ride the coach roofs
of locos to Delhi and hope to catch a ride west. But this is India, and the
slow trains are the only trains that cross the great plain of Punjab state.
Anything was better, one said, than drinking that rotgut bootleg rum
that the Hindis peddle in Khan market. No one, not one of them in
the twilight prison, had seen the Golden Temple.

## Finishing Work

The zinc roof sags,
a swaybelly'd horse.
But I saw the wood
across grain. At an age
when most are fathering
or saying I would never
do that again, I'm out
nailing down planks
against the inevitable day

when heaven falls,
when the fleet-of-foot
are overtaken, and rains
break through into baptism.

*I can count down to zero*

and measure
the distance between stars,
for distance poses no threat.
The chalk line's blue
lingers on the shingles
just above a finger
smudge of blood.

There's much to gain
by giving up,
but who would witness
my drowning in
material?

The whole day's a parade
in honor of the possible.

*The hammer a mind beating time.*

This coffee cup
hangs on an ionized nail
in a galaxy where
time begins again.

## Respect for the Dead

I live among these old masters,
with their curled capitals, words
that come up at you
and pass over your head,
a string of English-looking
phrases, a snake in Elizabethan
cross-dress—not a computer-generated
way of skipping through
the news of the day.

The paper blows away, down
Main, across the park to some tree
it wraps itself around like plastic
or a skirt, hugging the thing
it came from.

And I think, this is the historic
moment, soon lost in the currents
of a one-culture future,
the moment the wind
dies, and electrical lines
carry the flame, and the print
is cured into blackened wires.

And the news comes up
as a future injection,
a simple cure for reading, and time,
which no one has time for,
even to talk about. What, what
was that? And the dead
are walking around in the air
without the need of their eyes.

## Inside Wat Pho

This is not the simple absence of noise,
nor that absolute pressure in your ears,
it's not the jump of the heart,

but that silence that infect spaces
set aside for history. The Chinese lions
at the gate. The Thai gentleman in a top hat.

This composure is that of stones
forged in volcanic eruptions, which in turn
become islands, hissing as they join the sea.

Buddha's on his side, *reclining,* as if the word
were itself partially asleep. The figure
resting on an elbow like an Asian Atlas

only differently, holding up his head
and not the world, although still in the world.
This silence is audible, open like the mouth

of a cave. The shrine rests on the old city,
Ayuthaya. His gold body in quiescence. Visitors
deaf, or singing in low voices, mingling

histories. A smile like a sheen on wet stone,
hair the pattern of pebbles in the yard, soles
of his feet mother-of-pearl swirls

counterpoised with a turbulent world.
This is a silence that rings in your ears
as desire fills the sky with noise.

# Desert Fathers

*The desert had become a city.*
*—Athanasius of Alexandria*

Forty years looking for the face of God,
and sand storms will raise facial features,
the desert's phrenology, the mirage of gold

lake surfaces shimmering on the forbidden tar,
and out across the great expanse of *now*,
a faceless future.

The hermitage, a stack of stones, water
coming from the grace of sky, the snakes
more prevalent than sons of man,

make alchemy, seasons vanish. The truth,
whatever satisfies the mind, lies in the earth, a cinder
of eternity. More come to visit, more want

the name that does not take to letters,
the word that splits like a husk of dwarf corn
on the hard, flat surface of reality.

In wisdom, fathers fled the caves for higher
ground, dissolved into the air, let birds
pick at their heavenly bones.

And carried with them the loneliness of men
who have found nothing in an open hand.
The cities emptied, and desert caves filled.

That wisdom, like grains of sand, spilled out
along the edge of the universe, and stars
took up the cause, hot to form the race again.

# Reburial

*... "burial site" means any natural or prepared physical location,*
*whether originally below, on, or above the surface of the earth,*
*into which as a part of the death rite or ceremony of a culture,*
*individual human remains are deposited.*

—*Native American Graves Protection and Repatriation*
    *Act, 1990*

Behind the warp of glass,
a woman's skeleton curled
as a cocoon, or a fetus,
but dry as a turkey bone,
saved, an ant farm survivor,
on the other side.

She seems to desire nothing
but a private place to spend eternity,
and when she's moved, turned out,
she's reinterred in real ground.
As a boy, I wondered after her,

my own body flush with images
of death, the nature of unnatural
resurrections. She was always
my museum destiny carried past
the skeletal Tyrannosaurus Rex,

to papier-mâché mountains
and the primitive village site,
down the long corridor to stand
before those weathered bones,
thin as birds', her hair of twigs.

More transient than mine, her
dusty life, curled forever into
a question mark. Yet as I grew
she climbed to escape, when
someone remembered her name.

## The Irony Miner

He begins where others have left off,
deep in the mire, underneath the ground
with this helmet light showing him the way.
One of many, into his own heart

of darkness. He slips on his own blood,
spilled the day before, when he swung his pick ax
and punctured his leg. But he bleeds enough
for a whole company of miners, and still survives.

His children think he is a poor musician,
working for the mining camp. When they hear
the trombone's clear article of faith rising,
lifting itself awkwardly in the stillness of the night,

they sleep a little easier, believing he knows
not what is best but what is right.

# The Colossus of Rhodes

seems less magnificent today, in the postmodern
aftermath of history, for it has stood, straddling the harbor
only in some Einsteinian time, out there ahead of us
before an earthquake brought its rumor down.

It was never where they said it was, its shell,
the bronze of its massive arms and legs, and what then
of the genitals? The Greeks made them small, well-formed,
but still, where has the great metal phallus gone?

We sail into the harbor on the backs of dolphins
as the dead do in other places, and view only columns
mounted with stag and doe, the modern equivalent of care
with history, delicate rather than imposing.

If this beast of bronze never did exist, *The Seventh
Wonder of the World* would be a myth, and there's
more than something real in that, for writers, travelers
of the past, would have created our best hope.

But today, I see it, boy-eagled over the murky depths,
and the Japanese, Swedes, Germans, lingering
bankrupt Americans, all with their perfect daughters
and sons, snapping photos of the empty air.

## Running

Not always in the same
universe, the same spacetime
continuum, some

warp in the way bodies
regenerate, or refuse to,
and ankles, knees,

bones of the brain,
constantly fight
the seasons. For they are not

the same, not the same
spring in the step uphill
at heaven, nor in

the long miles
along trails that seem
rockier, more

personal, the weather
harsher than
forever.

Not the same
but sweeter maybe, legs
like *Chi Chi* sticks

tossed out
on *terra incognita*,
bones picked up,

grown strong by
being out there, thrust
and parry in air and earth,

singing against the end,
a runner's mantra,
next hill,

next curve,
life strung out,
a tensile thread

between coming and going,
and into the next
whatever

it can be,
long as it
carries you forward.

## Behind the Houses Under Construction

Where were we going with our thick cigars
and brutal individualities?
At night, we pushed my parents' car down
the block, to start across the city

to houses of girlfriends who were
even prettier in the dark. Hear that cranking
ignition? Where did we end on those night journeys,
coming to their houses in 3 a.m. fictions

of love? Was it a hot blindness of animal intuition,
something that would plague us all our lives?
Cigars got more common, and more expensive,
and we sat in city centers daydreaming lies

about the way things were, about the fools
mistaken for gods, and blissfully gulled.

# Gallarus Oratory, Dingle

The gulls have lost their way inland to the oratory;
no signs of that ancient defecation,
no crusts like snow on the corbelled slate.

The dry-stone arch like a boat's hull turned upside down
juts its spear into Heaven. Inside it is May,
salt air stirred by tourists plumbing time's darkness,

and coming up with nothing but stone.
A small, deep-set window over the absent altar space
for light and the flux of bodies moving in and out

create a stir and afterglow, atavistic conditions we believe
brought us to meditation. Climbing out the hole,
it's said, would save the soul. But how small it is,

how impossible to fit back into the world again.
More space among the speckled hills running to shoreline grasses.
The heart sounds are muted by heavy slate and Smerwick Harbor's

surf piled up by the rack of Atlantic winds.
Heart sounds muted like foreign horns playing the old songs.
The monks, monadic in their faith

were idiocratic in the spaces they would build for it.
Human traits betray a pride in perfect alignments, dry-stone
precision, the escape through that small, altar hole.

# The Call

> *And as they talked they perceived that a crow had settled on a*
> *branch of the tree, and softly flying down deposited a whole loaf*
> *before their wondering eyes. And when he had withdrawn,*
> *"Behold," said Paul, "God hath sent us our dinner..."*
>
> —St. Jerome's *Life of St Paul of Thebes*

What first hermits found, out there
beyond the desert's edge, back
when untracked seas of sand did not end

in telephone lines and asphalt strips
along Suez or Vegas oases, but merged
with the mind's measure of the universe,

the surface of the earth a true
dimension still, flush with the light
from a million recent stars,

was emptiness like a wardrobe,
the echo of each word until the word
tumbled into noise again. A palm leaf

covers Paul's more material self,
palm fruit his single sustenance,
if other than the wind, sand grit,

and fleas. The crow then saved him
in a myth shared by Celtic women warriors,
and Native Tricksters, laughing

as it released the sun, saved him
as the infant Dalai Lama was saved,
by crows, the same ones

who taught men how to bury their dead.
In the Coptic icon, he wears a bearded
scowl, driven mad by a thirst for things

that do not fall from heaven, things
cursed by us before we find them true.
Earthly things he baked into a loaf of bread,

the one the crow left, unselfishly,
tinkering with his soul to find out just how
men alone survive.

## The Other Side

Silence is often mistaken for an absence.
But it houses something. The skin drops away,
the world enters, and if there is not a jump
of the heart, or an absolute pressure

in your ears, it comes on anyway, comes from
the waiting other side, from who you are when you
are not counting minutes, calculating, bothering
to worry. It takes the contour of smooth stones

you have not yet stopped to pick up. On the tundra
of Iceland, it comes from stones forged
by volcanic eruptions, by the noise of islands
being formed. Here, it is a silence both of land

and sea, never completely one place
or thing. The birds break it up repeatedly,
like needles of ice, the noise sudden,
separate, from all that remains. Here, silence

is not above or beyond, not inside or out.
It is the quintessential element of the order
of the world. It is the animal we once were
crawling back toward the heart.

It brings up hot blood from the earth's core.
It grows in the bones. And it is only after
days or weeks that you suddenly know
it is something you can carry home with you.

## Last Chance Café

Some see it as the end of the road,
but then the road goes on,
perhaps into nowhere, into the sands
that wash away things somebody's tried

desperately to save. But last chance
places are always at the ends of things,
or at the beginnings. This café
with its half-hinged sign, its clouded,

sun-streaked glass, is just one place
where the universe turns a corner
into desolation, on a stretch of highway
no one can quite remember the name of.

If you buy sundries from the adjacent store,
they are brittle as dinosaur bones.
The museum has a two-headed snake
and plaster cactus stalks faded to lime green.

The formica table tops and stools
are patterned like grandmother's tablecloth.
And if you buy gas, it is the rusty,
sandy petroleum of the desert.

But if this truly is your last chance,
after all, it's only one last chance,
and if you survive you'll remember it
as an outpost of your future life.

## The Butterfly Effect

Once you say *I love you*
it rhymes with everything.

Ripples in the lake
begin to change your mind.

Of course, the mind
changes.

You have only to say
a word like *but*

and everything is up for grabs.

Then, on the contrary,
the world escapes.

That sudden storm
stirred by the fluttering of tiny wings

six thousand miles
to the north of you

is a lover's song
with a word left out.

A tin can falls from the sky
and clangs on a solitary earth.

It lands on a beautiful continent
you have only read about in books.

The world has come to an end.

The best time then
is when all is at risk.

It's then you cast yourself out
on the sea of cause and effect.

## Mystic Renovations

As if this mysticism were an old house,
I wander the helter-skelter of favorite furniture
like a child through the legs of tables and chairs
carved by a younger man. In crowded rooms,
the walls are empty, stained where the pictures
once hung, and there's nothing left to do
but clean. I start with the Queen Anne Victorian
gloom, renovate the American Modern,
cut the cobwebs from the dusty Gothic,
and dump the artifacts of a lost civilization.
Older now, I think of the space rather than
what fills it, like the distance from the sofa
to the T.V. The space there fills a lightyear,
a worm-hole through which so many lives
have slipped, only to be brought back
to this beginning of their end. I can see
the moon in daylight, shadows the sun casts
against my mountain. I can see stars
but they are further away now, more distant
than memory. Once, I could have traced out
the meaning of starlight on the back of my hand.
But where is that hand now? Where has
that body gone? The warp of time brings
half of me back into the presence of the past,
the other half is left behind in the now.
But that is only half-right, for I'm compelled
to keep cleaning the house that I have built.
Nothing of the grand cabala remains but
its candelabra swinging from a sagging beam
and the ideas that have not already fled
crammed into the storage shed of the self.

## Diorama

Memory loss housed in a kind of museum, where the dust (always dusty, no matter how diligent we are) collects on the animals like late winter snow, turns hard plastic plants to gray signatures. These are simply moments to look at, observe, walking through a secret interpretation of history, studying yourself under the mock natural lighting and behind the time-barriers of glass. We were told that once this was the way primitive humans looked, this papier-mâché image forever escaping the Mastodon, an extinct beast that will never move, surrounded by the monochrome people of this small, North American village. I came to know history as tableau, a page in a lost book, scenes that remind me only partially of what I cannot now remember: the others with me, the woman holding my hand. This truly prehistoric life, an appendage of my own experience, as if I lived here, stands perfectly still in the unnatural moment of real lives. Was I a warrior then, or a boy still, watching the crouching saber-tooth tiger, wondering after, rather than suspecting, the distant figure of a people crossing the desert? We traveled greater distances back then, under the umbrella of dead-blue skies without shadows. But with time, *in time,* in this particular room, the scene, the diorama, aberrant and unliving things, began to change. Revisionists work here, dismantling the plastic texts of history. I remember only a place that had never been, a view of a time that was purely mine and yet no one's. No one wants to forget, but we find in these reconstructions of the past a kind of rehearsal. Move an arm or leg, adjust a faded buckskin dress, almost feel the warmth of the electric flame, and we sink into the movements again, housings of loss, to live out a single day against the backdrop of eternity.

## Watching the Trains

I stand close to the tracks
to see if the beast will somehow
silently consume me in passing,
but what really moves is my body
as the sound touches my skin
and we become a portal for
something new to happen.
The Doppler is only an effect.
In the real world, the train
burns a time all its own, not only
the sound of something
shifting, wavering, growing
impossibly until it peaks
in the hollow of your naked ear,
but a revolution of the earth
where you stand watching,
your self in sudden parallax.
Some go up to Darlington
to watch the Stockton trains
come by the original short stretch
of rails, mimicking in locomotion
the first train, the first sense,
sound and flesh converging,
and then, like death,
leaving us behind.

# Landscapes

*We are subjected to the tyranny of objects...*
                 *—after Alexandros Mátsas, Rhodes, Greece*

Here, in the material landscape
of island paradise and sea, of sweat-shop
Barbie dolls and Bali silks
imported to such Greek isles, distributed

like grains of wheat, or milk, among
the starving tourists, the children
play by the shore they say is free of jellyfish
and moray eels, free to drown under a gypsy mother's eye

unhindered.

Perhaps we'll find ourselves here again,
along a coastline close to the Turkish fleet,
in the face of a sailor or in the guise of high-heeled girls
wandering the fortified city's mazy streets.

Whatever it is that finally hampers our movements,
we are molecules of this shared stuff, this new
material of the islands, and we will never
fashion ourselves differently

until one of us is born naked from the sea.

## Last Gas for A Thousand Miles

It's out there on the edge of things,
out past the café with its pink flamingos

next to the railroad tracks,
where the engineer stops on Wednesdays

to have a bite to eat, his engine sitting restless,
wheezing, at the knife-edge of the universe.

It's on the road mistaken for the road
from town, for no one comes this way,

the desert just beyond digests the living
in a mouth of sand, and sun seems to shimmer

on a vein of blood. Riding into the swayback
station, in leather spacesuit, chaps and goggles

glazed with a paint of insects, you see
the next dimension, a liminal storefront

simulacrum, light of stars and lights of towns
*just down the road* rising on the highway's

wet mirage. To survive this coming world,
you'll have to choose another mate,

a scorpion perhaps. Skin will fuse to bone
before you acclimate, the sky will drop

in tidal waves of rain, flushing arroyos clean
across your trail. It's said the insects grow

to giant science fictions. Your meek
five gallons galvanized by time, you're born

out on a flagellum of road, a new body of glass
fused from light and an ancient world of sand.

# Returning

*To return to the source of things,*
*one must travel in the opposite direction...*

—*René Daumal*

First, you must undye your hair
and get all that nasty brown out clean,
so that the gray seems a silver coronet
again, crowning your shrinking head.

Next, you must learn to walk upright
without that annoying cane, standing
straight as if in heroic stance, taking
that first step with rejuvenated legs.

Then you need to remember all that
the years have forced you to forget,
and know that others too will start
returning, undead, unborn, almost new.

Finally, you'll have to crawl back
into that strange woman's silent dream
and swim for your life, paddling upstream
into the heaven of having not been.

$\infty$

# Acknowledgments

I am grateful to the editors of the following publications where poems in this collection, sometimes in earlier versions, first appeared:

*Ranfurly Review:* "Learning to Swim"
*Dublin Quarterly:* "The Cannibals"
*Moulin Review:* "Modern Articles of Faith"
*Poetry International:* "The Hermits of Dingle"
*Osiris:* "Ice Hut"
*Quantum Poetry Magazine:* "The Greek Isle"
*Istanbul Literary Review:* "River Ice"
*Vox Humana:* "Hagiography"
*Lyons Recorder:* "Trails," "The First Music" (as "Music"), "Returning"
*International Zeitschrift:* "The Most Remote Prison in the World," "Teak"
*Penpoint View:* "Hands on the Wall"
*Ithacalit:* "Death Valley"
*Prairie Poetry:* "Ride"
*Atticus Review:* "The Poem Talks Back"
*Slow Train:* "The Poet's Hand," "Watching the Trains"
*Contemporary American Voices:* "Inside Wat Pho"
*Clockwise Cat:* "The Dali Café"
*Drafthorse:* "The Real Thing," "Subways in Europe," "The Poet's Place"
*Cartographie:* "Capela dos Ossos"
*Amarillo Bay:* "The Irony Miner"
*American Athenaeum:* "Survivor Suite"
*Blue Lake Review:* "The Far Side of Heaven"
*Semaphore* (New Zealand): "Respect for the Dead"
*Sawbuck:* "Junk"
*The Green Door:* "The Dogs of Calcutta," "The Old Man of Hoy"
*Glass:* "The Language School"
*Cavalier:* "The Sacred City"
*Criminal Class:* "A Night in the Life..."
*Autumn Leaves:* "In Another Country," "The Other Side"
*The Big Toe:* "Kathmandu"
*The Puritan:* "On the Death of Other People," "Every Day Poets," "Finishing Work"
*Cantaraville:* "The Monkey Temple," "Reburial"
*Frigg:* "From a Short Distance"
*Mayday:* "The Colossus of Rhodes"

*Angelic Dynamo:* "Behind the Houses Under Construction"
*Zone:* "Running"
*Caesura:* "Gallarus Oratory, Dingle"
*Assisi Journal:* "The Butterfly Effect"
*Orbis:* "Landscapes"
*Tonopah:* "A Geography of Heights," "Last Chance Café"
*Adirondack Review:* "Mystic Renovations"
*San Pedro River Review:* "Last Gas for a Thousand Miles"
*JMWW:* "The Monk's Body"

*Cover photo, "Skellig Michael," by George Moore; photo of the author by Tammy Armstrong Moore; cover and interior book design by Diane Kistner (dkistner@futurecycle.org); Adobe Caslon Pro text with Abril Fatface titling*

## About FutureCycle Press

FutureCycle Press is dedicated to publishing lasting English-language poetry and flash fiction books, chapbooks, and anthologies in both print-on-demand and ebook formats. Founded in 2007 by long-time independent editor/publishers and partners Diane Kistner and Robert S. King, the press incorporated as a nonprofit in 2012. A number of our editors are distinguished poets and authors in their own right, and we have been actively involved in the small press movement going back to the early seventies.

The FutureCycle Poetry Book Prize and honorarium is awarded annually for the best full-length volume of poetry we publish in a calendar year. Introduced in 2013, our Good Works projects are devoted to issues of global significance, with all proceeds donated to a related worthy cause. We are dedicated to giving all authors we publish the care their work deserves, making our catalog of titles the most distinguished it can be, and paying forward any earnings to fund more great books.

We've learned a few things about independent publishing over the years. We've also evolved a unique, resilient publishing model that allows us to focus mainly on vetting and preserving for posterity the most books of exceptional quality without becoming overwhelmed with bookkeeping and mailing, fundraising activities, or taxing editorial and production "bubbles." To find out more about what we are doing, come see us at www.futurecycle.org.

## The FutureCycle Poetry Book Prize

All full-length volumes of poetry published by FutureCycle Press in a given calendar year are considered for the annual FutureCycle Poetry Book Prize. This allows us to consider each submission on its own merits, outside of the context of a contest. Too, the judges see the finished book, which will have benefitted from the beautiful book design and strong editorial gloss we are famous for.

The book ranked the best in judging is announced as the prize-winner in the subsequent year. There is no fixed monetary award; instead, the winning poet receives an honorarium of 20% of the total net royalties from all poetry books and chapbooks the press sold online in the year the winning book was published. The winner is also accorded the honor of judging the next year's competition.

www.ingramcontent.com/pod-product-compliance
Lightning Source LLC
Chambersburg PA
CBHW070007100426
42741CB00012B/3146